Congratulations Bonnie & Greg !!!
What a great way to retire and see
the world !!!
Aloha from the most beautiful place on Earth !
AnneMarie 9/1/07

KAUAʻI

SPOUTING HORN

KAUA'I

SMITH'S TROPICAL PARADISE

KEĀLIA BEACH

KAUA'I

Photography by **Douglas Peebles**

Text by **Jan TenBruggencate**

Mutual
Publishing

Library of Congress
Catalog Card Number 2002108996

Book Design
Michael Horton Design

ISBN-10: 1-56647-574-0
ISBN-13: 978-1-56647-574-7

First Printing, November 2002
Second Printing, July 2004
Third Printing, June 2006
3 4 5 6 7 8 9

Mutual Publishing, LLC
1215 Center Street, Suite 210
Honolulu, Hawai'i 96816
Telephone (808) 732-1709
Fax (808) 734-4094
email: mutual@mutualpublishing.com
www.mutualpublishing.com

Printed in Korea

TABLE OF CONTENTS

KALALAU BEACH

PHOTOGRAPHER'S NOTE

I HAVE LIVED IN HAWAI'I FOR

over 25 years. My home has always been on O'ahu; however, I have come very close to moving to Kaua'i a couple of times. My first book was on Kaua'i and I have made more trips there than any other island. My next one will be in two weeks. It will be a camping trip down the Nā Pali Coast which I have done at least a dozen times before. I don't really keep count.

SELF-PORTRAIT

I have said the reason that I like to go back to the Island of Hawai'i is that it is different each time I visit. The reason I love Kaua'i is that it is the same. That is the beauty of it. I can count on the brilliant blues and greens of the ocean and mountains, clean beaches and clear water. Maybe this is because it is the oldest island and that makes it more resistant to change. I think this is true not just physically but politically as well. The people of Kaua'i, while as friendly as anywhere in Hawai'i, are a little more set in their ways and I believe this helps keep the island as it is and should remain.

I will be going back often.

Douglas Peebles

NĀ PALI SNORKELER

HIBISCUS

THE ISLAND OF KAUA'I,

with its neighbor Ni'ihau and the bird sanctuary islets Lehua and Ka'ula, lies alone within the island chain. Historian Ed Joesting called them a "separate kingdom." Except under remarkable atmospheric conditions, you can't see either of the islands up or down the chain—O'ahu to the southeast or Nihoa to the west. That makes it different from the other major islands, which have views across much shorter channels.

When Captain James Cook's ships pulled up at Waimea in 1778, the British crew could readily pick out Ni'ihau, just 17 miles away, but they were unaware that there were other islands in this group.

SEATED HULA, WAIMEA

The 60-mile Ka'ie'ie channel that separates Kaua'i from the major islands in the chain is so wide that it has three names. Perhaps it was to help navigators mark their progress. The Ka'ie'ie Waena is the middle of the channel, where the winds are largely unaffected by islands and the swells sweep cleanly from northeast to southwest. Ka'ie'ie Waho, the common name for the channel, means the outer Ka'ie'ie, and Ka'ie'ie Loko is the inner Ka'ie'ie. At its O'ahu end, the waves are steep as they cross the undersea shelf extending beyond Ka'ena Point. At the Kaua'i end, trade wind swells reflect off the island and create a confused sea. Even in misty conditions, or when caught in showers, navigators could use the sea conditions to tell which part of the channel they were sailing in.

KAYAKING OFF PO'IPŪ

CAPTAIN JAMES COOK STATUE, WAIMEA

The length and challenge of navigating the channel has played a singular role in the island's history. Kaua'i, while never entirely cut off, remained culturally distinct in certain ways. Its artifacts retained older

WAIMEA PIER

designs as the other islands modified the shapes of adzes and poi pounders—the stone implements used to mash the cooked corm of the Hawaiian staple, taro. Its language, too, retained older patterns. Even today, residents of Ni'ihau speak with a cadence and pronunciation of consonants that is reminiscent of the Polynesian languages south of the equator, while the main islands have moved more completely away from the old soundings. The most notable of these differences is the use of the letter "t" in some words that the rest of the chain pronounces with a "k" sound.

When the Napoleon of the Pacific, Kamehameha, set out to conquer the Hawaiian chain, his canoes were stopped by the Ka'ie'ie channel. Many were swamped and others turned back during his first invasion attempt. An epidemic of Western disease killed many of his

HULA DANCERS IN TRADITIONAL ATTIRE

4

SMITH'S LUAU ALONG
THE WAILUA RIVER

chiefs and warriors as his canoes rested on the beaches in preparation for his second attempt. Ultimately, he employed other methods, kidnapping the Kaua'i king, Kaumuali'i, and arranging the king's marriage to one of Kamehameha's own wives to cement the relationship—and the ascendancy of the Big Island Kamehameha clan over the traditional rulers of Kaua'i.

Today, the island continues to have a different feeling from many of the others. Geologically, it is 5 million years old, far older than the islands to the east. Rivers flow

NĀ PALI

in all directions from its central mountain mass. Erosion has cut deep valleys and has created rich soils that support dense vegetation. Its nickname, the Garden Island, makes perfect sense when you first view it.

Most of the island's towns date to the days when sugar was king. They are set around the fringes of the island. Too far inland, the land was too wet to till, the countryside too rugged. The main roads link town to town. There is no cross-island roadway, although increasing traffic on the perimeter roads may dictate one be created before long.

Tourism is settled in on three different coasts of the island, each with unique characteristics. The sunny, leeward south

CANE FIELDS

WAIMEA

coast, around Poʻipū, is noted for calm seas and dry weather. The east coast, from Līhuʻe to Kapaʻa, has regular breezes off the sea and is most active commercially. The north side, around Princeville and Hanalei, has amazing cliffs and mountains that you'll recognize from any of a dozen movies made there.

On the roadless Nā Pali, when the mists rise from the sea and mingle with the blade-like green ridges, a mystical feeling pervades. A separateness.

This island, it is easy to believe, floats alone in the Pacific.

WAIMEA TOWN CELEBRATIONS

PALI KE KUA BEACH

HAWAIIAN GREEN SEA TURTLE

Chapter One
PO'IPŪ TO POLIHALE

THE WEST SIDE OF

the island has a special feeling about it. It has plantations, ranches, calm blue water and older communities. It has tree-lined streets, board-and-batten houses, home-built solar hot water heaters and four-wheel drive vehicles. Its shops are tucked into the old buildings of rustic sugar towns—like Kōloa, Hanapēpē and Waimea.

This side of the island has been defined by its sugar plantations over the past two centuries. Sugar started here at Kōloa in 1835. The remains of one of the old stone sugar mills are a historical feature smack in the middle of town. That mill's fields stretched eastward into the limestone of ancient exposed reefs and the deep brown eroded valleys of Māhā'ulepū, and westward to the wetter valleys of 'Ōma'o.

KEKAHA SUGAR COMPANY MILL

The sugar fields themselves supplanted evidence of an older culture, where Native Hawaiians had diverted water out of the streams onto the hard black lava. They presumably brought in soil and lined their waterways with clay, and grew crops on this hot, sunny landscape. Within the Kiahuna golf course property and on the neighboring Kukui'ula project, developers were required to preserve special historic sites, including old stone house sites, agricultural terraces and waterways.

KAUA'I COFFEE PLANTATION

This is a complex environment, and beneath the rocks of Kōloa and Po'ipū lies evidence of even earlier inhabitants. In the lava tubes and cracks there is a unique dark environment, in which rare insects live out their entire lives without

KŌLOA TOWN

SPOUTING HORN, PO'IPŪ

ever seeing light. A little shrimp-like amphipod lives off the dying roots of surface plants. And a blind hunting spider—its eyes evolved away after countless generations in darkness—preys on it. Both of these creatures are included on the national list of endangered species. In all the world, they are found only under the lava rocks and in the limestone cracks and caves of this region of Kaua'i.

WAIMEA TOWN CELEBRATION

In a limestone sinkhole at Māhā'ulepū, researchers have studied pollen and concluded that this entire region was once forested with native plants. Many of them, like the amphipod and the hunting spider, were found nowhere else in the world. Unfortunately, their habitat was in demand, and all obvious signs of the ancient dryland forest are gone.

Today, tourism is the leading employer of the region. Sugar has gone the way of the dryland forest, the lava creatures, and the Hawaiian farmers of centuries past. Truck farmers on old sugar land produce fine lettuce and asparagus that are served up on dinner plates at the hotels. Tiger Woods and the other icons of golf play the links built around old Hawaiian stone walls. Tourists shop for trinkets in shops where plantation workers once bought their bags of rice, the lunch pails called kaukau tins, and the ubiquitous fabrics of the time: plaid palaka and denim.

West of the resort area, Lāwa'i Valley, a historic green gully that is now home to the National Tropical Botanical Garden, was once overlooked by a vacation cottage of Queen Emma, one of Hawai'i's favorite members of royalty during the 1800s. The hills of Kalāheo rise from the edge of the valley. The old volcanic cone that forms Kukui o lono was said to be the site where large fires were lit to guide fishermen home from ventures far out to sea. These green hills are popular today for cool homesites, but the region was once more noted for its cattle pastures and garden plots. Portuguese immigrants brought Isabella grapevines from the island of Madeira, and planted them on these slopes to make wine.

KEONELOA BEACH / SHIPWRECK BEACH

Steep rocky cliffs line the sides of Hanapēpē Valley. From the lookout at the side of the highway, high Manawaipuna Falls are hidden. They are known to moviegoers as the waterfall in *Jurassic Park*. Helicopter pilots tour the region, some of them calling the cataract Jurassic Falls.

Hanapēpē was once the island's economic center, home of the major harbor, and the commercial airport. Both have been supplanted by facilities closer to Līhu'e, but the town's quaint architecture still draws visitors, especially to its cluster of art galleries. And out on the peninsula that still houses the old airport, Hawaiian families still pour salty water into earthen pans, evaporating them to make sea salt that is prized for cooking and ceremonial functions.

BARREL RACING

The last remaining sugar plantation on the island is the Gay & Robinson plantation, a conglomeration of predecessor companies' fields and equipment. G&R was once the smallest of the island's plantations and it had no sugar mill, selling its crop instead to a neighboring firm. But during the 1990s, it bought out Olokele Sugar Co. and acquired the firm's sugar processing factory. And, with the turn of the century and the close of its other neighbor, Kekaha Sugar, it leased several thousand acres of that company's land. The firm has a small museum in the village of Kaumakani, and it gives tours of both the factory and the sugar fields.

Across the island's largest river, the Waimea, begins an economy driven by technology and diversified agriculture. The old sugar fields that weren't taken over by G&R are growing crops that include shrimp, hogs, and several kinds of plants grown by seed companies. Residents can drive by rows of corn, soy, sunflowers, and other crops that are being grown in experimental plots or to create seed for the vast agricultural areas on the mainland.

PO'IPŪ COAST

PO'IPŪ

But the coastal area past Kekaha, along the Mānā flats, is the site of the Pacific Missile Range Facility, where the United States conducts fleet training exercises and tests new missile and anti-missile technology, optical sensors, and other equipment. A cluster of defense contractors has office space in Waimea town to serve the needs of the missile range.

One of the most impressive features of the region is a white-sand beach that stretches more than 10 miles from Kekaha around the missile range to Polihale, a state beach park. The road ends here, and the rugged Nā Pali Coast begins.

WINDSURFING AT MĀHĀIEPŪ

HANAPĒPĒ SALT PONDS
Following pages

PO'IPŪ

KAUMAKANI UNITED METHODIST CHURCH 19
Following pages

KŌLOA SUGAR MILL

MALUHIA ROAD TO POʻIPŪ

MAKAWELI SUNSET

PĀKALĀ PLANTATION VILLAGE
Following pages

POLIHALE BEACH

HĀʻUPU MOUNTAINS

LĀWAʻI VALLEY

PUʻUWAI, NIʻIHAU

NIʻIHAU

LEHUA ISLAND OFF NIʻIHAU

HULA DANCERS

CASCADES POUR INTO

the Waimea Canyon from the vast Alaka'i Swamp and, with each rolling stone, with each landslide, the canyon gets wider. It is an incredible lesson in geology, with ancient lava flows displayed edge-on, dating back millions of years. The iron-rich reds and oranges, basalt blacks and grays, the pale aluminum-rich rock and soil, all create a rainbow of earth tones. The canyon has been compared to America's Grand Canyon.

The lands to the western side of the canyon fall away from the canyon rim toward Nā Pali, "The Cliffs," which

HULA DANCERS

form the northwestern edge of the island. The curving road that runs along the western edge of the canyon provides myriad vistas, both from formal lookouts and from simple roadside wide spots. Only one formal hiking path, Kukui Trail, runs down the side of the eroded west wall to the river below, but hunters and long-time residents know of other ways in and out. Residents sometimes hike or ride horses into the canyon from the canyon mouth at Waimea town. Old trails provide avenues into the canyon from the eastern side, but they are often poorly maintained and ill-marked.

Except for hikers and hunters, Waimea Canyon is deserted today. But there is plenty of evidence of past use. Early Hawaiian residents farmed here, and their stone-lined taro paddies can still be seen deep in the highest valleys. One sign of former habitation is the presence of bananas and ti plants. Since the early Hawaiian varieties of banana and ti did not seed, their presence proves someone came here and planted them.

KALALAU LOOKOUT

In the canyon's lower reaches is the mysterious waterway known to some as Menehune Ditch, and to others as Kīkī a Ola. It is unique, because the stones that form the ditch walls are cut to shape. Except for stone statuary, such worked stone was virtually unknown among Hawaiians. The ditch still carries water today, feeding the taro fields of present-day Hawai'i residents in Waimea Valley. Many island residents refer to the upper reaches of Waimea as the canyon, and the lower areas as the valley.

KŌKE'E BIKE RIDE

In the forested areas above the canyon lie the Kōke'e state park and the Alaka'i Swamp. At elevations from 3,000 to more than 5,000 feet above sea level, they cover some of the most stunning collections of native wildlife remaining to be found in all the Islands. The state park is readily accessible at the top of the road that runs along the canyon. Numerous trails lead off in various directions, some down the ridges of Nā Pali, some along the edge of the canyon, and a few out into the swamp.

Alaka'i has been called the world's highest swamp. At nearly a mile above sea level, it is under near-constant cloud cover. Flat bogs have formed throughout its 8-mile length. These are places where volcanic ash has turned to clay, preventing the frequent rains from seeping into the soil. Plants in the bogs are often stunted, and hikers are treated to the sights of flowering adult trees that are only knee-high. But the bogs are also occupied by plant species that are unique to this ecosystem. Native orchids, sedges and lobelias abound. Tiny flycatchers, known in Hawaiian as miki nalo, spread out tiny arms supplied with small hairs, each of which has a glistening drop of sticky fly bait on it.

Sometimes, while hiking in the swamp, you'll come across other visitors carrying little bottles or cameras with

HULA KUPUNA

WAIMEA CANYON WATERFALL

HULA PERFORMANCE

macro lenses, notebooks and magnifying lenses. Scientists are regular visitors here. They study all facets of the swamp, from its geology and plant life to insects, snails and birds.

For birds, the Alaka'i and other high forests represent the last refuge in the Islands. Many of the archipelago's native birds have gone extinct, driven over the edge by habitat change, predation by humans and other animals, and diseases. In the high forests, there has not been much direct habitat alteration, and often the mosquitoes that bear diseases like avian malaria and pox are kept at bay by the chill temperatures.

So here, high in the woods, you can see the scarlet 'i'iwi with its long orange bill, the pert 'elepaio with its tail upturned, and, if you're lucky, hear the warbling of the small Kaua'i thrush, the puaiohi. This bird's population, which is down to a few hundred individuals, is limited in range to one or two valleys of the island's uplands. It has been the subject of a successful experiment in captive breeding and reintroduction. Scientists associated with the San Diego Zoo, The Peregrine Fund, the state Division of Forestry and Wildlife, and other agencies collected eggs from nests here in the wild. They hatched and raised the chicks in captivity, allowed them to mate, and raised another batch of chicks. Many of those chicks have now been reintroduced into the Kaua'i forests, where they have mated—either with each other or with wild birds—and produced young. The indication of the success of the project is that there are now more puaiohi in the wild that have come through the captive rearing process than the number of eggs originally taken.

The story is not always so rosy, however. One of the most prized birds of the Hawaiian forest was the ʻōʻō. Different varieties of this bird were once found on different islands. Each of the ʻōʻō was a slate to black bird, with yellow leg feathers and yellow feathers under the wings. Hawaiians collected the feathers to adorn prized capes and helmets worn by chiefs. But even after the collecting of the birds ended, the numbers of these birds declined. The last known hatching was of a bird deep in Kauaʻi's Alakaʻi Swamp in the 1970s. The last time an ʻōʻō call was heard was in the 1980s. They are now believed to be extinct.

MANAWAIPUNA FALLS

HULA PERFORMANCE

While the high walls of the Waimea Canyon and the bogs and valleys of the Alakaʻi are less affected by human activities than other parts of the island, the impact of the human presence is growing. Wild pigs, the results of crosses between native pigs and European animals, tear up the forest floor. Mosquitoes seem to be adapting gradually to higher elevations. Alien plant species and alien birds are invading the deepest parts of this refuge.

When you visit the region and notice stately conifers, know that they are alien. Blackberries along the road, alien. Red fuchsias and the green kikuyu grass, alien. The vines with pink downward-facing blossoms hanging from giant koa trees, the banana poka, alien. Hawaiʻi's native species are being asked to compete against the most aggressive plants on the globe and, as occurs in any isolated landscape, they're losing.

WAIMEA CANYON

ALAKA'I WILDERNESS

KAWAIKINI

MANAWAIPUNA FALLS

PĀʻŪ RIDER

WAIMEA CANYON

HULA

HULA DANCERS

'ŌHI'A TREES IN THE KŌKE'E FOREST

IPU

OLOKELE CANYON

WAIʻALEʻALE CRATER

KALALAU LOOKOUT

WAIMEA CANYON

BIRD OF PARADISE

Chapter Three

LIHU‘E TO KĪLAUEA

SAILORS SEE WHAT

appears to be a great dark pyramid as they approach Kaua‘i from O‘ahu across the Ka‘ie‘ie Waho Channel. It is the end of the Hā‘upu mountain range, which sweeps westward into the island's interior from this rugged point on the eastern side. Nāwiliwili Bay and harbor are protected on the south by this range, and the Hulā‘ia River runs along its base. Native Hawaiians explained the rugged terrain inland from the harbor and along the base of the mountains in mythic terms. Here was an area where the god Kamapua‘a, taking the form of a giant boar, tore up the land with his tusks while pursuing the fire goddess, Pele.

SMITH'S LUAU

**RIVERBOAT ON THE
WAILUA RIVER**

One of the significant features of this region is a wide fishpond, built within a bend in the river. It is the Alakoko pond, but is most commonly known as the Menehune Fishpond. According to one of the stories of its construction, a chief and chiefess, who were brother and sister, arranged for its construction with the Menehune, the mythical small people of the Islands, who were known for their prodigious public works. The Menehune agreed to build the pond, and would do so at night, as long as they were not watched. The brother and sister could not help themselves, and, during the night, they climbed up from the back side of the Hā‘upu range to spy on the Menehune. The story is that they were immediately turned to stone. Today, if you stand at the lookout over the pond and look up at the ridge, you can see two low bumps on a side ridge leading toward the river. They are the remains of the chiefly couple.

CHRIST MEMORIAL EPISCOPAL CHURCH

WAILUA RIVER CRUISE BOAT

Visitors arriving by air will view a quarter-mile-long white-sand beach backed by 10-story hotel towers. They are the island's only high-rise buildings. The first two towers were built as part of the Kaua'i Surf Hotel, and the third, when the hotel was rebuilt as the Westin Kaua'i. The property is now known as the Kaua'i Marriott, which combines hotel and time-share vacation ownership functions. Alongside is the Kaua'i Lagoons property, whose two 18-hole golf courses are built around 40 acres of interconnected man-made lakes.

Uphill from the harbor and resort area is the town of Līhu'e, the island's commercial and political center. Primary government offices are here, as is the airport and the largest shopping center. The old sugar plantation that was the town's founder has closed, although its old sugar milling factory still lies at the junction of the two highways that circle most of the island.

There is considerable residential property around Līhu'e and the neighboring hamlets of Hanamā'ulu and Puhi, but the bedroom community of the island is the Kapa'a-Wailua area. Most of the commercial activity in this region remains along the coast. A volcanic spine whose Hawaiian name is Nounou backs the region. But it is popularly known as the Sleeping Giant. If you view it from the sea side, you can faintly pick out the Giant's reclining figure. The uplands beyond the mountain form a broad, moist plain

slung between here and the island's central mountain mass. The area is mostly devoted to housing. Just half a century ago these flats were mainly pasture
and pineapple fields.

Wailua River, which flows between the Nounou and Kālepa mountain
ranges, was among the most culturally important parts of the island in the
years before Western contact. Chiefs lived here, enjoying the rich bounty of the
seaside, as well as the cultivated lowlands along the river. In rough water, they
could fish from inland ponds that are now part of the Coco Palms resort. Their
sons and daughters were born at the base of a giant stone outcropping not far
from the river. Hawaiian temples marched from the seaside up to the island's
center at Wai'ale'ale. Here, at an elevation near 5,000 feet, alongside a natural pool near the island's highest point, the outlines of the uppermost temple are
still visible. Some of the lower religious and cultural areas are protected within the state's Wailua River State Park.

Kapa'a town is a sprawling commercial zone that has grown out along the
highway from a center near the old pineapple cannery on the grounds of
what's now a condominium apartment complex. This region was once low and swampy, and plantations cut canals to
drain the water and make some of the land arable. Entertainer Bette Midler has bought some 1,400 acres of the lowlands

WAILUA RIVER

PUHI

KĪLAUEA LIGHTHOUSE

running from town up to the Sleeping Giant, and proposes the restoration of some of the wetlands as habitat for native waterbirds. The state has five native waterbirds, of which four are endangered. Only the Hawaiian black-crowned night heron, or 'auku'u, is still common. But it's not too difficult in lower wet areas around the island to locate the others: the Hawaiian duck or koloa, coot or 'alae ke'oke'o, gallinule or 'alae 'ula, and the stilt or ae'o. Kaua'i has more surviving ground-nesting birds in large part because the mongoose, which is found on the other major islands, never became established here.

A reef protects the Kapa'a beaches, and provides prime conditions for kite surfing. When the wind blows hard, athletes zip across the water, often becoming airborne as they use waves as launch ramps.

WAILUA RIVER STATE PARK HEIAU

The coastline moving north from Kapa'a is a rugged windward shore. There is a wide sandy beach at Keālia, where sunbathing can be great, but, as is the case around the island, swimming can be treacherous when the waves are up. Here, the highway leaves the shore and cuts inland, along abandoned sugar and pineapple fields. The village of Anahola is primarily a Hawaiian Home Lands settlement, where Native Hawaiians are provided with land for housing and agriculture at low cost. The bays and headlands beyond Anahola, on the northeast brow of the island, are a mixed economic bag, from the old family homes and beach houses of the tiny bayside community of Moloa'a to large, exclusive private estates.

COCONUT TREES AT WAILUA
Following pages

WAILUA BEACH

WAILUA FALLS

PĀPAʻA BAY

WAILUA BAY
Following pages

63

KAPA'A

FERN GROTTO

NĀWILIWILI HARBOR

KALAPAKĪ BEACH

WAILUA RIVER

LĪHUʻE

KEĀLIA BEACH
Following pages

KAUA'I LAGOONS

MALAE HEIAU

HAWAIIAN MONK SEAL

SLEEPING GIANT

MOKU'AE'AE ISLET

WAILUA FALLS

'ŌPAEKA'A FALLS

Chapter Four
HANALEI AND THE NORTH SHORE

THE NORTH SHORE OF

Kaua'i is dominated by Hanalei and its broad bay, one of the largest in the Islands. But this, the green windward side of the island, has many other wonders, as well. At the North Shore's eastern end, Kīlauea is a former plantation town now dominated by small farmers, retirees and folks who work elsewhere but prefer to live in the rural atmosphere of the old sugar town. Seaward of the town is a rugged shore of cliffs and offshore islands. Kīlauea Point is the northernmost spot in the main Hawaiian Islands, and was established as one of the main lighthouse locations in the territory, to warn ships passing through the

HANALEI PIER

North Pacific of the dangers of these shores. A small corps of Coast Guard personnel once lived on the point to maintain the lighthouse, but, once the light was automated, they were not required. However, wildlife officials had noted the remarkable birdlife of the area, and the land was transferred to the Department of Interior, becoming the Kīlauea Point National Wildlife Refuge.

HANALEI RIVER

Here, seabirds that range across the entire North Pacific come to roost and nest. Birds abound here year-round, and their aerial acrobatics are readily viewed from the lookouts around the point. One of the most exciting scenes is to see great frigatebirds attacking other species in flight, to get them to disgorge fish being brought to nestlings. The prey birds will often drop their catch, and the frigatebirds will dive to snatch the morsels out of the air.

Nesting wedge-tailed shearwaters and Laysan albatrosses can often be viewed close-up. The birds evolved nesting on

KĒʻĒ BEACH, HĀʻENA

islands without humans or other mammal threats, and they seldom react to a person's presence. In addition, they don't defend themselves effectively against dogs, which is why the preserve has established an extensive fence system to keep stray pets out.

Princeville Ranch manages much of the undeveloped land between Kīlauea and Hanalei for cattle production. An associated company, Princeville Stables, gives horseback riding tours on the North Shore pastures and to hidden valleys and waterfalls of the region.

HANALEI BAY

Along the shore, the wide reefs of ʻAnini, once known as Wanini, protect the coastline. These are some of best beaches on the island for casual snorkeling, and windsurfers like the flat water and regular winds here. Weekend polo matches are often played on the big field across from the beach.

The Princeville resort is built on a 1,000-acre plateau that overlooks Hanalei Bay and the North Pacific. It includes golf courses, a hotel, time-share apartments, condominium complexes, a shopping center, and more. Next to the hotel are the earthen remains of a Russian fort built by traders in the late 1810s, as they sought to gain a foothold in the Islands. Another fort, the stone Fort Elisabeth, stands along the Waimea River, and is in better repair. The Russian effort failed,

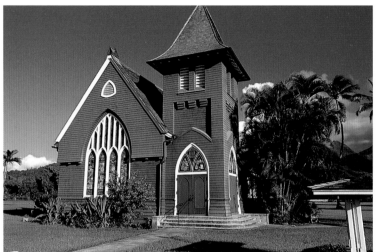
WAʻIOLI HUIʻIA CHURCH

apparently from a combination of lack of support from the Czar's government, and opposition from the Hawaiian chain's king, Kamehameha.

Hanalei Bay is a safe harbor only during the summer months. Small boats can take refuge inside the Hanalei River, but the sailing ships of old and the pleasure yachts of today normally leave the bay during the winter. The Hanalei tradition is that it's a safe place to keep your boat only between Memorial Day and Labor Day, and local boats hold races on those weekends, from Nāwiliwili to Hanalei at the beginning of the season, and back to the safety of the protected eastern harbor at the end.

The bay faces directly north, and the several valleys that feed into it are kept green by frequent rains. The valley bottoms are flat and fertile, and Hanalei is the state's biggest producer of taro, the most important food crop of the early Hawaiians, and one still prized today.

The taro ponds are also excellent habitat for native waterbirds, and several hundred acres of the valley bottom are part of the Hanalei National Wildlife Refuge.

The one-lane steel bridge one crosses to enter the valley is

HANALEI

86

nearly a century old, and badly rusted. The community has resisted the construction of a new, wider bridge for fear it will bring in more traffic, including tour buses, and will change the traditional character of the place.

Beyond the coastal Hanalei Town, the highway wanders in and out of valleys, along green cliffs, and across more one-lane bridges. A series of stunning beaches lines the coast.

Near the end of the road at Hāʻena are the Limahuli Gardens, a valley botanical preserve operated by the National Tropical Botanical Garden. It emphasizes plants used by early Hawaiian residents, and the original native ecosystem of the region.

The pavement ends at Kēʻē beach. Here is a protected small lagoon and white-sand beach, ancient temples, and the beginning of the trail that leads to the incomparable Nā Pali.

QUEEN'S BEACH

HANALEI VALLEY

HANALEI

HĀʻENA

LUMAHA'I

SAILING CANOE ALONG THE NĀ PALI

KĪLAUEA POINT LIGHTHOUSE

PRINCE COURSE AT PRINCEVILLE

HANALEI VALLEY
Following pages

101

Chapter Five

NĀ PALI COAST

THIS COASTLINE,

an army of marching ridges and valleys, cloaked in greenery and flecked with bare rock faces, at first glance appears impenetrable. But the region had two important features that led Hawaiians to extended efforts to gain access. One was that its very impassibility made it highly defensible. Many of the valleys are called hanging valleys, since they end at a cliff that drops into the sea, instead of in a beach at sea level. Another attraction was that the regular trade winds brought ample rainfall to the northern end of the coast, providing permanent streams and springs that made agriculture easy, once the tortuous terrain was overcome.

A system of trails, some of them now lost to disrepair and landslides, once connected almost all the habitable valleys.

The trails were by necessity rugged. In some locations they followed cliffside ledges formed by old lava flows. Sometimes they were cut manually out of weathered clay hillsides. In one location, on the trail around the cliff promontory between Nu'alolo Āina and Nu'alolo Kai, the route leads from one ledge to another at a different elevation. A ladder was rigged between them. The holes that were chipped into the basalt to provide lashing points for the ladder are still visible. Along the cliff face between Awa'awapuhi and Honopū, there is a break in the ledge used for a trail. An old log had been dragged perilously along the trail to span the break, providing a continuous walkway. It was visible into the late twentieth century, when it rotted and collapsed.

NĒNĒ GEESE

HONOPŪ ARCH

At its northern end, the famed Kalalau Trail begins alongside the beach at Kēʻē. It rises quickly in elevation, and, just a quarter-mile along the path, hikers can find one of the most impressive viewing spots looking down the coastline. Two miles down the trail, it returns to sea level at Hanakāpīʻai Valley, where coffee was grown commercially in the 1800s and the remains of an old coffee mill are visible. Camping is allowed here by permit. The white-

NĀ PALI COAST

sand beach is attractive, but the ocean at this beach, like those along the whole coastline, is treacherous. A rapid current along the coast, undertows generated by onshore surf, hidden rocks and ledges can all threaten the safety of swimmers. Even waders can be dragged into the ocean by unusually large waves.

Beyond Hanakāpīʻai, the trail remains well above the ocean as it feeds in and out of wet valleys, past the campsite in Hanakoa Valley, and eventually down the red clay slope into Kalalau itself.

Outrigger canoes were the preferred means of hauling passengers and cargo along the coastline in the Islands. The point of the trail system was to provide access during those frequent times when the ocean on the northwest side of the island was too rough to allow outrigger canoes to launch and land.

DOLPHIN

TI PLANT

There were fishing communities here, like those at Miloli'i and Nu'alolo Kai, but most of the valleys were used as taro plantations. In some valleys, virtually every square foot of valley bottom was terraced. Taro was grown in flooded ponds, with complex irrigation systems that routed stream water to each paddy.

As stunning as these agricultural systems were, they are overwhelmed by the power of the cliffs that give the region, all of which is part of a state park, its name.

Nā Pali: "The Cliffs." Most of the real estate in this park is vertical. Its turrets and pinnacles, its cathedral walls and narrow hanging valleys, its knife-edge ridges and plunging waterfalls are perhaps the most breathtaking sights in the Islands.

The largest of the valleys is Kalalau, and it is hard to say whether it is more impressive viewed from inside or out. Visitors can look down on it from a pair of viewing platforms along the Kōke'e Road, or on helicopter tours of the island. Coastal boat tours provide a view from below. But people who have walked in along the rugged 11-mile trail tend to have a unique sensation about the place, which many refer to in religious terms.

The Native Hawaiian residents of the valley left nearly a century ago. Cattle were ranched here for a time. Fifty years ago, a young physician took up residence alone for several years in a coastal cave. He was called the Hermit of Kalalau, and he gained a certain notoriety as a curiosity publicized by newspaper and magazine writers. He eventually left the valley, although he would return quietly to the island from time to time until his death.

When the state government acquired the land and made it a park, the old trail was improved a little, and the hike to Kalalau became a kind of pilgrimage for many. Some people, from ascetics to marijuana growers,

NĀ PALI COAST

took up illegal residence in campsites established in the valley. They are routed out on an irregular basis by state rangers. The demand for Kalalau is so great that the state established strict limits on the number of people who can camp in the place at any one time—no more than a few dozen—to protect both the resources and the visitor's experience.

Several of the valleys of Nā Pali are prohibited for public access, to protect their unique archaeological and botanical treasures. The only place beyond the Kalalau trail where camping is allowed is Miloliʻi, although day use is permitted at Nuʻalolo Kai.

NĀ PALI COAST SUNSET

The remarkable valleys of Honopū, Awaʻawa-puhi and Nualolo ʻĀina are left to the goats.

At a glance, it would seem that this must be one of the most protected native habitats on the globe. It is not. The botany of the coastline is threatened by alien weeds, by the loss of pollinating birds and insects, and by goats. Goats eat many of the native Hawaiian plants, which are particularly vulnerable because they evolved without grazing animals around, and tend to have few protections against them. Goats also promote erosion because of their aggressive feeding.

The steepest cliffs are the most protected parts of the coast, because, in some cases, even sure-footed goats can't get to them. Here, botanists using helicopters and rappelling techniques, collect seeds and pollinate some of the rarest plants in the world.

NĀ PALI COAST SUNRISE

KALALAU VALLEY

HĀʻENA

PORPOISES OF THE NĀ PALI COAST

KALALAU VALLEY
Following pages

NU'ALOLO KAI

NĀ PALI CLIFFS

SOUTHERN END OF NĀ PALI

HONOPŪ ARCH

KALALAU STREAM

NĀ PALI COAST

KAYAKER'S VIEW

KALALAU TRAIL

HANAKĀPĪʻAI VALLEY

KALALAU BEACH

WILD TARO

FISHING FOR ʻŌPAE SHRIMP

HONOPŪ ARCH

KALALAU BEACH

Page iv/v The widest beach between Keālia and Anahola is popularly known as Donkey Beach, since a plantation once pastured its donkeys near here. Its Hawaiian name has been lost, although some call it Kūnā Beach and others give it the name of the nearby point, Palikū.

Page viii A Kalalau Beach sunset, seen through the mist, creates a rainbow.

Page 1 Nā Pali snorkeler.

Page 1 The famed Spouting Horn east of Po'ipū erupts when a wave enters a coastal lava tube that has an exit through the overlying lava rock shelf. A unique feature of this blowhole is that an accompanying hole allows a small amount of pressurized air to escape, causing a moaning sound, said to be the voice of a mythical lizard caught under the rock.

Page 1 Pu'upōā Beach, Hanalei.

Page 2 Hibiscus, National Tropical Botanical Garden.

Page 2 A sunset kayak ride along the south coast of the island at Po'ipū provides an opportunity for visits with pods of porpoise and, in winter, with whales.

Page 2 Seated hula, Waimea.

Page 3 The statue of discoverer Capt. James Cook gets special adornments each year during the Waimea Town Celebration, which started as a footrace called the Captain Cook Caper.

Page 4 After a race, canoe paddlers haul their six-seat outrigger from the calm waters off Waimea, next to the Waimea Pier.

Page 4 Hula dancers in traditional attire.

Page 5 Visitors watch ancient hula performed at Smith's Luau along the Wailua River, with the dancers' images reflected in the pond that lies between entertainers and audience.

Page 5 A lone set of footprints speaks to the remoteness of the white sand beaches of the Nā Pali.

Page 6 A few years ago, sugar fields pushed to the edge of this road north of Po'ipū, but now pastures and cattle have taken their place.

Page 7 Kids with horse, Waimea.

Page 7 The annual Waimea Town Celebration celebrates Hawai'i's diversity, here with hula, but also with rodeo, canoe paddling, footraces, and lots more.

Page 8 The sands of this quiet beach at the base of the Princeville cliffs lie at the base of the Pali Ke Kua condominium project. It is known alternately as Pali Ke Kua Beach and Hideaways Beach. A private access is through the condominium property.

Page 9 A Hawaiian green sea turtle glides over the reef off Hā'ena. Most female turtles lay their eggs in shallow holes in the sand on atolls in the northwestern Hawaiian Islands, and return to the main islands to feed. Green sea turtles are vegetarians, feeding almost exclusively on seaweed.

Page 10 Coffee fields, seen here near Kalāheo, are part of Kaua'i Coffee's plantation, on land that once grew sugar. The firm's more than 4,000 acres of the caffeine-rich crop form the largest coffee plantation in the United States.

Page 10 Hawaiian flag on horseback.

Page 10 A horse grazes on a coastal lawn near the old Kekaha Sugar Co. mill, whose stack is a navigational icon for fishermen off the west side of the island.

Page 11 The old sugar town of Kōloa was the birthplace of the sugar industry in Hawai'i. The first sugar plantation was started here in 1835. The stone remains of one old sugar mill stand in the middle of town, alongside a sculptural memorial to the crop.

Page 12 From Po'ipū's view of Spouting Horn at sunset, the blowhole looks much like a humpback whale exhaling on the horizon.

Page 12 Cowboys check out the competition at the annual rodeo that is part of the Waimea Town Celebration.

Page 13 The remains of an old wooden hull are long gone, but Keoneloa Beach still retains the popular name, Shipwreck Beach. The translation of its Hawaiian name is "the long sand."

Page 13 Cutting it close at a barrel race during a Po'ipū rodeo.

Page 14 Jim Miranda leads a group of horseback riders along the Po'ipū Coast.

Page 14 A throw net fisherman stands as still as a statue, watching a school of fish in the nearshore waters at Po'ipū.

Page 15 When the trade winds whip around the southern side of the island, Māhā'ulepū becomes heaven for those who love coastal windsports. Windsurfing and kite surfing are popular activities of the region.

Page 16/17 Hundreds of years ago, Hawaiians poured salty water into shallow clay pans, letting it evaporate in the sun to make salt. Today, their descendants still carry out the tradition on the peninsula fronting Hanapēpē town, known to residents as the Salt Pond.

Page 18/19 Cottages and condominium apartments line the coastline at Po'ipū, their appearance softened by the coconut palms that thrive along the shore.

Page 20/21 A tasseling sugar cane plant in the foreground sets off the serenity of a modest plantation church under the palms near Kaumakani. The Kaumakani United Methodist Church was the first Methodist church on the island.

Page 22 The old Kōloa Mill, seen here before it was closed, served three different sugar plantations during its long career. It was initially part of the Kōloa Sugar Company, which was later purchased by Grove Farm Company. Grove Farm, in turn, leased the mill and some of the firm's sugar lands to McBryde Sugar Company, which closed its sugar operation in 1996.

Page 23 The Tree Tunnel on Maluhia Road is a double line of *Eucalyptus robusta* trees, providing drivers with a shaded treat as they approach or leave sunny Po'ipū.

Page 24/25 The west side of the island competes with Hanalei for the best sunset viewing on the island. At Makaweli, the sun prepares to dip behind distant clouds before disappearing under the horizon.

Page 26/27 The old coastal plantation village at Pākalā is one of the last plantation-owned housing complexes on the island. The reef fronting the beach attracts dozens of surfers when swells come from the south.

Page 28/29 The last beach on the west side of the island, Polihale, is a state park and forms the southern end of the Nā Pali coast. Its dunes back the widest beach on the island.

Page 30 The shape of the clouds atop Hā'upu Mountain changes with the weather, but some form of cloud is almost always present. The mountain range is viewed here from a Po'ipū golf course.

Page 31 Lāwa'i Valley was a vacation home for popular Queen Emma during the 1800s, and during the middle 1900s was the retreat of Chicago millionaires Robert and John Gregg Allerton. Today the valley is home to the National Tropical Botanical Garden.

Page 32 The village of Puʻuwai on remote Niʻihau lies on a white-sand beach on the far side of the island from Kauaʻi. Residents here see no lights on the horizon when they look out to sea.

Page 33 Niʻihau, viewed from a boat at sea, is a low island lying in the lee of Kauaʻi's mile-high central mountains. The island's geographical alignment means the trade winds drop most of their showers on Kauaʻi. Niʻihau, as a result, is generally quite arid.

Page 33 Lehua Island, off the north side of Niʻihau, is a volcanic tuff cone with a crescent shape that protects a small, deepwater bay. It is a state wildlife reserve for the protection of monk seals that haul out here and the seabirds that nest on the island.

Page 34 The view from the Kalalau Lookout at the end of Kōkeʻe Road looks though verdant forest vegetation down toward the coast. Clouds often form in the valley and blow up to the lookout on the winds that whip in from the sea.

Page 34 Traditional hula garb.

Page 34 Preparing for performance.

Page 35 The view over the handlebars is breathtaking, but perhaps not as exciting as the bicycle ride itself, down from Kōkeʻe, dropping some 3,000 feet in elevation.

Page 36 Many hula demonstrations are danced to music played by old-timers, known as kūpuna, who pass on the ancient traditions of the Islands to youngsters.

Page 36 Skirts sway with the athletic movements of the dance.

Page 36 Waimea Canyon waterfall.

Page 37 A helicopter banks to give right-window passengers a view of Manawaipuna Falls.

Page 37 Hula blues.

Page 38/39 The deep erosion of Waimea Canyon cuts into the broad, flattened shield shape of the ancient volcano that formed Kauaʻi. Geologists date the formation of the island to about 5 million years ago.

Page 40/41 A waterfall punctuates the deep forest in this view of the Alakaʻi wilderness of central Kauaʻi. Streams flowing out of the Alakaʻi form the headwaters of all the island's major rivers.

Page 42 The summit of the island is Kawaikini, which means "the many waters." Between Kawaikini and nearby Waiʻaleʻale, deep in the heart of the island, countless waterfalls drain into the island's valleys.

Page 43 Manawaipuna Falls were made famous in the movie, *Jurassic Park*. The waterfall lies in a branch of Hanapēpē Valley, but is not visible from the roadside valley lookout above ʻEleʻele.

Page 44 Riders in colorful attire on decorated horses are traditional features of Hawaiian parades and festivities. The broad skirts worn by the women are called pāʻū, and the equestrians are often called pāʻū riders.

Page 45 Formal lookouts have been built at some of the best views along the rim of Waimea Canyon, which visitor publications call the Grand Canyon of the Pacific.

Page 46 A key to the movement of the bodies in the hula is the power of the ankles, which are often adorned with wreaths of leaves and flowers.

Page 47 Young dancers often spend far more time in the mountains collecting greenery and blossoms for their hula than they actually spend performing.

Page 48 Mists roll through the ʻōhiʻa trees in the Kōkeʻe forest. Rain brings most of the moisture to the forest, but fog drip, created when the mists condense on leaves, are also a factor.

Page 49 Gourds are used to provide percussive accompaniment to hula, often being both pounded on a mat and tapped with the hands.

Page 50 Olokele Canyon is one of the several valleys that spread out like compass points from the center of the island. Water here flows from the edge of the Alakaʻi Swamp, through this narrow valley, and joins the Waimea River just a mile above the shoreline.

Page 51 Near the summit of the island is the pool known as Waiʻaleʻale, or "rippling water." It gives its name to the ancient crater, seen here under the clouds, which many believe is the heart of the volcano that formed the island.

Page 52 Viewed from the Kōkeʻe forest, Kalalau Valley is the broadest of the Nā Pali coast valleys and once supported the largest population among all the valleys of this region.

Page 53 Geologists believe that the Waimea Canyon is the result of a massive fracture that tilted the western end of the island toward the sea. The resulting fissure was expanded through erosion to create one of the state's most visited sights.

Page 54 Bird of Paradise.

Page 54 The riverboats that ply the Wailua River provide visitors with Hawaiian music, legend and tours of the Fern Grotto, a vast cave draped in greenery. It is a favorite spot for wedding ceremonies.

Page 54 Hula performers at Smiths Tropical Paradise.

Page 55 A classic stone front sets off the old Christ Memorial Episcopal Church building in Kīlauea. Stonework using boulders collected in the sugar fields are an architectural hallmark of this community.

Page 55 A Wailua River cruise boat—actually a barge pushed by an attached power module—makes a turn in the state's biggest navigable river.

Page 56 Near Puhi.

Page 56 Kayakers paddle up the Wailua River. While the ocean can often be dangerous for small craft, the major threat to folks cruising the rivers is sunburn.

Page 57 The old Kīlauea Lighthouse is maintained as a historic treasure, but, these days, the actual light is an automated beacon that stands beyond the old concrete building with its prismatic lens.

Page 57 Several Hawaiian religious structures, called heiau, are protected within the Wailua River State Park. Wailua was once the home of the island's chiefly class and one of the most sacred parts of Kauaʻi.

Page 58/59 Coconut trees were once part of the Hawaiian agricultural industry. The dried meat from the coconut was called copra and was sold for its high oil content. Today coconuts like these at Wailua are more valuable as backdrops for the visitor industry.

Page 60/61 Wailua Beach seen through the trunks and fronds of coconut palms on the south side of the Wailua River. Structures in the distance, across Wailua Bay, are the condominium projects of the Waipouli coast.

Page 62 Wailua Falls drops over the face of a cliff in three sections, each fed by a separate channel in the rock river bottom above. The waterfall was used in one of the opening scenes of the television series *Fantasy Island*.

Page 63 Isolated Pāpaʻa Bay lies on the eastern shore of Kauaʻi. The shoreline is protected by reefs, but has a small channel that will allow the entrance of small boats to a protected anchorage.

Page 64/65 Wailua Bay faces east, toward the rest of the main Hawaiian chain, and toward the sunrise. Tradition tells of voyagers in ancient times who arrived here in canoes from the South Pacific.

Page 66/67 Sugar cane fields, seen here near Kapaʻa, are becoming a rare sight in the Islands. Once there were dozens of sugar plantations on several islands, but at this writing there were just two remaining, one on Maui and the other, the Gay and Robinson plantation, on the west side of Kauaʻi.

Page 67 A cavern alongside the Wailua River, known for its curtain of ferns and other vegetation, is known as the Fern Grotto. Tour boats regularly run up the river to the site.

Page 68 Several cruise ships weekly pass through the entrance to Nāwiliwili Harbor, seen here from the Marriott Kauaʻi Beach Resort. Nāwiliwili is the island's main commercial harbor, but it is also home to sailboat races, canoe paddling and fishing.

Page 69 The quarter-mile length of Kalapakī Beach, fronting the Marriott Kauaʻi Beach Resort, is all that remains of a long white-sand beach that once marked the perimeter of Nāwiliwili Bay. Most of its length has been sacrificed to landfilled harbor facilities.

Page 70 The Wailua River cuts between the north end of the Kālepa Range and the southern side of the Nounou, or Sleeping Giant. Its fertile lowlands were once a major taro-growing region.

Page 71 Līhuʻe, whose name was imported from a region of central Oʻahu, is the economic and government center on the island. It sits a mile east of the sea on a broad plain that is protected by mountain ranges on the south, west and north.

Page 72/73 The developer of the plateau north of Keālia donated to the county nearly three miles of coastline, including the small bay known as Donkey Beach. Its Hawaiian name is no longer known for certain.

Page 74 The golf courses at Kauaʻi Lagoons overlook the entrance to Nāwiliwili Bay and the foot of the Hāʻupu mountain range. Viewed from here, the sun rises over the sea, and sets over the island's mountains.

Page 75 The Malae heiau, a prehistoric Hawaiian religious structure, was invisible under a cover of weeds and trees until volunteers recently cleared it. It stands overlooking Wailua Bay and the Wailua River.

Page 76/77 Near Līhuʻe, Hanamāʻulu Beach Park is a popular recreational area.

Page 78 In recent years, Hawaiian monk seals have been hauling out to rest on Kauaʻi beaches with increasing frequency, as here at Wailua. The animals come ashore to rest, and to find protection to one of their main natural enemies, sharks. They are protected under federal law, and should not be approached. Besides, they bite.

Page 79 The Nounou mountain range is more familiar to most as the Sleeping Giant. In this view, the reclining image's face is at the left, with its forehead at the mountain's highest point and its chin just to the right.

Page 80 Mokuʻaeʻae islet in the foreground is a nesting ground for seabirds. It sits directly off the northernmost point of the island, Kīlauea, which is the site of an important lighthouse for ships in the North Pacific, and is also a national wildlife refuge.

Page 81 Daredevils sometimes leap from the top of Wailua Falls 200 feet into the pool below. Many of them have been killed, generally from internal injuries caused on contact with the water below. Physicians have said the injuries can mimic those of a high-speed car crash.

Page 82/83 ʻŌpaekaʻa Falls, another of the island's roadside waterfalls, drops from the southern edge of the Nounou mountain range. Shortly after dropping over this cliff, the ʻŌpaekaʻa Stream flows into the lower reaches of the Wailua River.

Page 84 The odd Brighamia plant, native to the cliffs of the Nā Pali region, is on the federal endangered species list. It is irreverently called "a cabbage on a stick." This specimen grows at the Limahuli Garden on the island's North Shore.

Page 84 The Hanalei River provides green vistas and quiet paddling for kayakers. The river leads past dense stands of hau trees, along pastures and taro fields and under the historic Hanalei Bridge.

Page 84 The old Hanalei Pier is a concrete monument to the days when crops like rice and sugar grown in the valley were taken out to freighters from small boats loaded here. Today, it is a popular place from which to view Hanalei Bay and the mountains beyond.

Page 85 The view across Hanalei Bay from under palms growing by the beach.

Page 85 Kēʻē Beach, Hāʻena.

Page 86 Hanalei.

Page 86 The old Waʻioli Huiʻia Church in Hanalei, on the mauka side of Kūhiō Highway, is one of the classic architectural features of the Hanalei community.

Page 87 Queen's Bath at the base of the Princeville plateau is a quiet refuge when the water is calm, but, in high seas, it can be deadly, pulling the unwary off the rocks and dragging them out to sea.

Page 88/89 Kauapea Beach west of Kīlauea Point is protected by cliffs and is sufficiently isolated that many visitors consider it clothing-optional, over the objections of neighbors and county officials.

Page 90/91 Hanalei Valley is the largest taro-growing region in the state. The taro plants grow in shallow water, which keeps weeds down and provides excellent habitat for several species of native waterfowl.

Page 92/93 The Princeville resort community is built on a plateau facing the North Pacific, but many parts of the area look across Hanalei Bay, where the sunsets are legendary.

Page 94 The coconut, seen here with a Hanalei sunset as backdrop, is not native to Hawaiʻi. The first Polynesian settlers introduced it. It provided food, fiber and shelter to the early residents.

Page 95 Juvenile fishes often swim in the protected shorebreak, like this one at Hāʻena, where a shallow reef robs oceans swells of the power to pound the beach. Occasional swirls in the water mark the presence of predators chasing the fry.

Page 96/97 The beach in the foreground, at the eastern end of Lumahaʻi, was made famous in the movie *South Pacific*. It's where Mitzi Gaynor sang that she was "gonna wash that man right outa my hair." The pandanus forest along the coast may represent the way this region looked long before the first humans arrived in the Islands.

Page 98 In the days of the early Hawaiians, the primary means of transportation along Nā Pali was canoes, which could be rigged either for paddling or sailing. Some residents, like long-time Hanalei canoe coach Nick Beck, still use them, though today it is mostly for recreation.

Page 100 The northernmost lighthouse in the state, Kīlauea Point Lighthouse is now also the center of a national wildlife refuge for the several species of seabirds that nest and roost here. In addition to the birds, visitors can often see Hawaiian monk seals, schools of porpoise and, during the winter, whales in the coastal waters.

Page 101 Golfers on the Prince Course at Princeville are treated to links hidden in dense vegetation, and to views that include waterfalls, mountains and the sea.

Page 102/103 Hanalei Valley's well-irrigated bottom lands were originally developed for taro, but two generations ago, rice was grown here, and a historic rice mill is still maintained in the valley, along the river. Today, taro is back in cultivation.

Page 104 Helicopter, Honopū Arch.

Page 104 Native beach vitex, pōhinahina.

Page 104 State wildlife officials have reintroduced the native Hawaiian goose, the nēnē, to the Nā Pali valleys.

Page 105 A kayaker paddles through a waterfall in a coastal cave along the Nā Pali, one of the highlights of a cruise through this wonderland.

Page 106 Nā Pali with dolphin.

Page 106 Ti plants, Kalalau Trail.

Page 107 Below the great amphitheater of Kalalau, campers sometimes pitch tents in the shelter of the shrubbery at left, but others prefer the protection of the sea caves to the right.

Page 108 A sunset view down the Nā Pali Coast displays the rough surf that helped erode the island's northwest face, creating dramatic sea cliffs. In many areas, the sea has cut caves into the base of the cliffs, making protected nesting areas for seabirds known as noddies.

Page 109 The waters off the Nā Pali are often calmest in the early morning, as here at dawn. Later in the day, the trade winds often kick up the ocean's surface, making navigation less comfortable.

Page 110/111 Kalalau Valley was populated by native Hawaiians into the early 1900s, but its isolation—it is only accessible via an arduous hike, or by boat during summer—led residents to move closer to civilization.

Page 112 The amazingly abrupt ridges of Hāʻena rise from a narrow coastal strip that gets considerable rain. Early Hawaiians sometimes climbed these cliffs and tossed burning branches off the peaks. The flaming sticks, caught on the rising winds, created a unique kind of fireworks display.

Page 113 One of the most fascinating features of boat rides down the coast is the array of wildlife. Porpoises, as here along the Nā Pali coast, often ride the bow waves of boats.

Page 114/115 During wet weather, many waterfalls appear on the high walls of Kalalau Valley, all feeding its main stream, seen here. The stream flows year-round.

Page 116 Coral reefs and waters that are protected in most weather conditions make Nuʻalolo Kai a favorite spot for boaters to take a rest, and for snorkelers to inspect marine wildlife.

Page 117 The wrinkled cliffs of Nā Pali drop abruptly from the flat uplands of Kōkeʻe. Elevations drop from near 4,000 feet at the back of Kalalau Valley to sea level.

Page 118 Nā Pali's southern end, most of it in the lee of the trade winds, is dramatically drier than the north side, which is regularly drenched by trade wind showers.

Page 119 The twin beaches at Honopū Valley are separated by a ridge whose base has been worn away by the sea and the Honopū Stream. The Honopū Arch is a favorite backdrop of movie directors.

Page 120 Balancing interesting stones atop each other is a favorite activity on rocky shores, as here at Kalalau.

Page 120 Stone balancing in midstream at Kalalau Valley.

Page 121 Kalalau Stream flows to the sea among boulders that have been worn both by rolling down the stream and by rolling in the shoreline surf. The source of the rocks is the lava flows eroding out of the valley walls.

Page 122 Visitors, enrapt by the scenery, cruise calm morning waters along the reefs, cliffs and valleys of Nā Pali.

Page 123 The view over the nose of a kayak provides one of the best vistas along Nā Pali.

Page 124 The Kalalau Trail winds in and out of valleys, and switchbacks up and down steep valley walls on its way from the beach at Kēʻē to the beach at Kalalau Valley.

Page 125 The only coastal stop along the Kalalau Trail between its start and its end is at Hanakāpīʻai Valley. Two miles in from the trailhead, it is a popular turning-around point for casual hikers not prepared for the 11-mile full trek.

Page 126 The beach at Kalalau ebbs and flows with the seasons. During winter the beach is narrow and a rock coastline is exposed, but in summer the sand covers most of the boulders along the valley's southern coast.

Page 127 Although the old taro paddies have been overgrown and water systems broken down, some taro still grows wild along the streams of Nā Pali, left from the days when this was the coastline's primary crop.

Page 128 Hawaiian streams have several edible native species, including fish, shrimps and snails, which can be trapped by those with patience and experience.

Page 129 Campers at Kalalau work together in the stream to find snacks in the form of tiny native shrimps called ʻōpae.

Page 129 A Kalalau Valley camper holds out his hands with the native freshwater shrimp, ʻōpae. The shrimps are plentiful, but some of the other stream species, particularly some kinds of native goby, are endangered.

Page 130 In Honopū Valley, a waterfall drops onto one side of the famed Honopū Arch, and the stream flows through the rock structure to the beach on the other side.

Page 131 Kalalau Beach, viewed from on high, on a calm sunny day.

Page 136 Sunset through the coconut palms at Hanalei Bay displays the clouds over the mountains behind Hāʻena.

Aloha

SUNSET AT HANALEI BAY